VEGETARIAN AIR FRYER COOKBOOK

A Stunning Collection of Perfect Healthy Recipes to Easily Fry, Bake, and Grill Your Everyday Vegetable Meals

Garry Goodman

LEGAL & DISCLAIMER

TABLE OF CONTENTS

INTRODUCTION

People always seek for diets that will help them maintain a healthy body and fit figure, but that will also keep them full.

Finding a good diet that offers healthy and tasty foods sometimes can be a challenge, especially if you want to lose some weight.

There are many diets that are promising you to successfully lose weight within three or five days. Usually, these diets will starve you, and your body will lose a few kilograms.

The truth about it is that once you go back to your regular ways of eating, your weight will return.

Starving yourself is never a good idea. It is a shock for your body, and a terrible way to see visible results.

In fact, you should never believe those diets that are promising you to lose weight in five days. That is the unhealthiest way.

If you decide to slim, find a healthy diet that will help you get rid of the extra kilograms within a reasonable time and while you eat healthy nutrients.

In this book, I want to share with you a diet that is a go-to food regimen for millions of people around the world.

Call it a plant-based diet, a vegetarian diet; it is up to you.

The vegetarian diet is a diet where you restrain yourself from eating meat (poultry, pork, beef) but still include animal products such as eggs, dairy, occasionally fish, and sea food.

What is so good about this diet?

First of all, people who become vegetarians are not eager to eat dead animals. The reasons can be many (ethical above all, but there are some people who avoid meat because of healthy reasons, others because find meat expensive).

The good thing is that you are always providing your body with fresh food that mainly grows from the ground.

And when your food is fresh and mainly plant-based, you can't go wrong.

Of course, meat itself is not the reason for obesity. Sugars, carbs, processed foods, and lack of physical activities are the main culprits for having a few extra kilos.

In this book I will try to explain all the important information you need to know about this diet, how it can help you lose weight, what benefits it will bring you and what foods are suitable for your meals.

I hope I got your interest so far.

If you are looking for a healthy way to change your eating patterns and become more compassionate with ever sentient being, let me guide you into the first chapter.

WHAT IS VEGETARIAN DIET? TYPES OF THIS DIET

The vegetarian diet is a diet that excludes eating meat (pork, poultry, beef) and includes mainly plant-based foods (fruits, vegetables, seeds) but also dairy products, eggs, and occasionally fish and seafood.

There are various reasons why people become vegetarians: for some, health is the biggest reason, for others religious beliefs, ethical reasons (some people don't want to feed on the expense of someone's life). Others prefer to avoid meat because of the involved antibiotics and hormones in it, or because they care for the environment (slaughterhouses add for the pollution just like regular factories). Some people follow this diet because the meat is expensive.

And while in the past it was believed that becoming a vegetarian is a luxury (meaning you will have to buy fancy foods to get protein substitutes and having to starve in the winter months when there aren't many fresh vegetables and fruits), today things are changed.

This diet is accessible, the markets offer fresh foods all year round, and there are more vegetarian options than ever. Vegetarian menus, restaurants and snack bars are everywhere.

Studies show that there are no health concerns when it comes to a vegetarian diet. Maybe in the past, people believed they wouldn't be able to get the needed nutrients for a healthy life, but today plant-based diet is recognized as nutritionally sufficient and also as a way to lower the risk for many chronic illnesses.

According to the American Dietetic Association, if you are carefully planning your vegetarian diet, you are providing yourself with healthy meals every day. This diet is wholesome, nutritionally suitable, and will give you the health benefits in the form of reduced cholesterol, lower weight, reduced risk of cardiovascular diseases, and boosted immunity.

Becoming a vegetarian is not difficult.

This diet should not scare you because you can eat vegetarian pizza, drink a soda drink, and eat your favorite candies. But, if you want to lose weight you will have to be smart and careful when it comes to the quality of your vegetarian food; you will want to eat more vegetables, fruits, and avoid processed foods.

You will have to substitute saturated and trans fats with healthy fats (avocado, nuts, olive oil).

At the end of the day, it is important to have limited calorie intake and exercise, if you want to slim healthily.

To do this, you will have to change your old eating habits, but also, you will have to become more mindful of the ingredients you are consuming.

If you are afraid that you will not be able to give up on meat completely, you can start slowly.

You can start involving a few vegetarian meals per week. In between meals instead of snacks, you can start eating fruits, vegetables or nuts, and substitute your regular cooking oil with olive oil.

Include plant-based proteins such as tofu, or eat fish instead of meat a few times a week.

This way, you will test the waters and see if this diet will work for you in the long run.

If your primary goal is weight loss and a healthy lifestyle, then the vegetarian diet will do an amazing job.

These is the main info you need to know about this diet – it excludes meat, poultry, and even fish (although some vegetarians do consume it).

There are several types of vegetarianism, and each of them has its own restrictions.

Here are the most popular types:

Lacto-vegetarian – it restrains fish, poultry, meat, and eggs but allows dairy products.

Lacto-ovo-vegetarian – it restrains fish, meat, and poultry but allows dairy products and eggs.

Ovo-vegetarian – there is no meat, fish, poultry, and dairy products, but you can eat eggs.

Pescetarian-vegetarian – Meat and poultry are eliminated, but you can eat eggs sometimes, fish, and dairy products.

Flexitarian – This is mainly a regular vegetarian diet that allows meat, fish, or poultry occasionally.

Vegan – Meat, fish, eggs, poultry, and dairy products are out of the question as any other animal-derived products like honey.

The Centers for Disease Control and Prevention tells that more than 65 percent of American adults are overweight, but the predominance of obesity among vegetarians and vegans is under 10 percent. On average, the body weights in both male and female vegetarians are 3-20% lower than omnivores.

Research shows that switching to a healthy plant-based diet helps in weight loss, even without lowering the calorie intake or regular exercise.

Studies have found a reduction of calories after vegetarian/vegan meals; plant-based foods are excellent fuels for the body, compared to foods that make the body store the fat in layers around the stomach, legs, arms, and back. However, you need to know that an imbalanced vegetarian diet will not keep you slim.

WHY YOU NEED TO START THE VEGETARIAN DIET?

Before I start writing about the health benefits of the vegetarian diet, I want to be clear that my mission is not related to convincing you that meat-eaters are wrong. I intend to show you how a plant-based diet can improve your health.

If we compare two people, one of them a meat eater and the other a vegetarian, the vegetarian tends to eat less saturated fat and foods that increase cholesterol. Also, a vegetarian is provided with a more massive amount of vitamins (C and E) as well as folic acid, potassium, dietary fiber, magnesium, and phytochemicals (plant chemicals) like carotenoids and flavonoids.

Thanks to the vegetarian diet, a vegetarian is more likely to have lower cholesterol and lower blood pressure, as well as lower BMI (body mass index). These three are associated with the risk of chronic diseases as well as longevity. However, it is essential to mention that consuming healthy plant-based meals is not the only thing that will provide you with a healthy life. Also, it is crucial to work out regularly, live a stress-free life, quit smoking and drinking, and be psychologically in a good place.

This is what we know from the medical researches so far:

Heart disease

Vegetarians have a lower risk for cardiac diseases (mainly heart attack) and death from heart failures.

In a study published a few years ago, that involved more than seventy thousand participants, on average the vegetarians had a 25% lower risk of dying from heart failures

In another study with more than sixty thousand participants (mainly people in the Oxford cohort of the European Prospective Investigation into Cancer and Nutrition (EPIC-Oxford)), the vegetarians had a 19% lower risk of death from heart issues.

If you want to keep your heart in good health, the best thing is to eat whole-grain foods and legumes (high in fiber). Such foods keep the blood sugar levels in balance and reduce the levels of cholesterol.

Nuts are an excellent food for the heart. They contain a low glycemic index and multiple antioxidants, fiber, vegetable protein, minerals, and good fatty acids. On the other hand, nuts are packed in calories and should be consumed in small amounts. But the great thing is that even a small amount will keep you full.

For example, walnuts are rich in omega-3 fatty acids, known for their numerous health benefits.

Fish is the best source of omega-3 fatty acids (which in some of the vegetarian types of diet is allowed). But, plant-derived omega-3 fatty acids may not be the ideal substitute for fish.

Cancer

Regularly eating fruits and vegetables will lower the risk of developing malignant diseases such as cancer. There is no scientific evidence that the vegetarian diet will protect you from this illness. Still, hundreds of studies show that the vegetarian diet will provide you with the daily needed servings of vegetables and fruits.

According to the Oxford Vegetarian Study and EPIC-Oxford, fish-eaters had a lower risk of certain cancers than vegetarians who don't consume fish at all. You can give up on meat for a while (no matter if you want to become a vegetarian or not), and you will reduce the risk of colon cancer. Vegetarians are known to have a lower risk of consuming foods that will remain cancerogenic substances in their colons.

Type 2 diabetes

Plant-based diets are known to reduce the risk of type 2 diabetes. Vegetarians are not as exposed to the risk of this illness as non-vegetarians are.

According to the Harvard-based Women's Health Study, there is a link between eating red meat (mainly processed meats – hot dogs, bacon, and salami) and diabetes risk.

Bone health

As women age, their bone health tends to get weaker. Osteoporosis is widespread (bones are exposed to a higher risk of fractures). This is why some women are not prone to switching to the vegetarian diet. The reason for that is that the vegetarian diet is reducing the number of dairy products, which are the primary source for healthy bones.

If the health of your bones is your priority, you can always pick one of the types of vegetarian diets, such as lacto-ovo vegetarians (where you are allowed to consume dairy products and eggs). This type of vegetarian diet provides you with enough calcium (almost as much as a regular meat-eater gets on a daily basis).

According to the EPIC-Oxford study, vegans (the strictest type of the vegetarian diet) get less than the recommended daily amount of calcium and have a higher rate of fractured bones.

Besides dairy products and eggs, some vegetables like broccoli, bok choy, Chinese cabbage, kale, and collards are rich in calcium. Also, Swiss chard and spinach contain calcium, but they are not the best choices because, besides calcium, they contain oxalates that make it harder for your body to absorb the calcium.

Fruits and vegetables that are rich in potassium and magnesium are excellent for reducing the blood acidity, which will lower the risk of the elimination of calcium through the urine.

Vegetarians (particularly vegans) are at higher risk of not getting enough amounts of vitamins K and D that are needed for bone health. Some leafy greens do contain vitamin K. If your choice is veganism, you should include leafy greens in your diet, as well as organic orange juice, rice, and soy milk and cereals, as well as taking the vitamin D supplement.

WILL THIS DIET HELP YOU LOSE WEIGHT?

No matter what type of diet you are following, it is essential to know that the weight loss will start when you reduce the number of calories. This is why it is important to consume fewer calories compared to the number of calories that you burn.

If your intention is to lose some weight, you will have to cut your calories and combine that with regular working out sessions during the week.

Perhaps some diets are created to help you slim fast, but it does not mean that they are good for your health.

Losing weight at the rate faster than one kilogram per week is not a healthy option. First of all, it will be a shock for your body, and second, your weight will return once you start eating like you usually do (the infamous yo-yo effect). Let's say that your goal is to slim healthily while eating wholesome meals that contain everything your body needs (proper amount of proteins, fiber, carbs, and fats) and that you don't lose more than one kilogram per week. To maintain this, you will have to reduce your calorie intake. Your healthy meals should include vegetables, fruits, nuts, healthy fats and fatty acids, olive oil, water, organic juices, and a limited amount of carbohydrates. Besides that, you can combine your vegetarian diet with restricted calories with a combination of physical activity. Just like in any diet, water is essential; it will keep you hydrated and will help your digestion.

The easiest way to create a good combination of your nutrients is to create the 40-30-30 split. This means that you get 40 percent of your calories from carbs, and proteins and fats come in 30 percent each.

As mentioned before, a vegetarian diet ranges from lacto-ovo (where you can eat dairy products and eggs) to veganism, which restrains every food from animal sources (no meat, dairy, eggs, fish, even honey). One thing I want to add here is that vegetarians are naturally leaner than meat-eaters, thanks to the diet that does not contain saturated fats and is mainly focused on whole foods, fruits, vegetables, and grains (which do not contain a high amount of calories). Vegans consume even fewer calories and fats since they do not eat anything that comes from animals. Their diet is strictly plant-based.

This is why they can quickly lose weight.

But, every person has a different body, and this diet will not necessarily bring the same results to everyone.

If you are switching to vegetarianism because you want to lose weight, make sure you listen to your body and how it reacts to the plant-based meals. Talk to your physician and a nutritionist; they will tell you what foods will work for you the best.

Set goals that will be easy to achieve, instead to start with harsh goals, where you will starve yourself and shock your body.

The crucial thing is to be disciplined; it is the key to every weight-loss process. The vegetarian diet is not a low-calorie diet. There are many vegetarian foods and meals that are packed in calories. So, if you are not careful or disciplined, don't be surprised when your weight does not go down.

Every change takes courage, discipline, and dedication. This means that once you switch to vegetarianism because you want to lose weight, you will have to keep your eyes on the prize.

Now you will have to be more aware of the ingredients you use (a product that contains numerous ingredients is most definitely packed with unhealthy nutrients). The fewer ingredients a product has, the healthier it is.

Let's take, for example, one of those instant mac and cheese packages. Sure, they are tasty; they belong to the vegetarian palette and do not require some special cooking skills. But, the ingredients show that they contain various cheese mix, sodium, citric and lactic acid, and so on. In the long run, eating such foods will not help you slim down (this is a processed food rich with carbs).

So, it would be smarter to prepare the meal by yourself, instead of getting it from a box. Also, eating out can be a little challenging because you can hardly control the calorie intake in a restaurant.

If you want to lose weight, you will have to be careful about your portion sizes. If you are used to large portions, you will have to reduce the amount of food you eat. This is the first step towards cutting your calorie intake.

The best way to do this is by planning your meals in advance. Preparation of meals (one night before, or preparing your entire weekly menu) will save you time and nerves, but also it will be a good way to be sure that you are eating balanced meals with lower calorie intake.

Planning is a crucial part of any weight loss regimen, no matter if you are vegetarian, vegan, or a meat-eater.

Also, how you prepare your meals is important; focus more on steam cooking, baking and boiling, instead of frying.

No matter what diet you are following plant-based or meat-based, it will not do the job one hundred percent, if you are not active. Working out regularly will make your body stronger and will define your muscles. Also, it will help you digest your food easier and faster; when you give your metabolism a boost, it will be easier for your body to eliminate the extra weight.

The great part about exercising is that you can decide what works best for you. You can go to the gym, start practicing yoga or Pilates, cycle, or simply hike or walk whenever you can. Seek suitable workout programs that are made especially for vegetarians (some workouts are focused on bodybuilding that requires animal proteins).

A good way to start is walking to work or school, or use the stairs instead of the elevator. You can even workout at home (at least today, we have an endless number of free videos and workout applications).

TIPS TO LOSE WEIGHT WHILE EATING VEGETARIAN FOOD

Every healthy diet, no matter if it is plant-based or contains meat, should contain healthy nutrients – proteins, carbohydrates, fats, and fiber.

The vegetarian diet does not contain meat; therefore, the protein sources are not going to come from animals. But, plants, dairy products, and fish do contain proteins, so vegetarians are not in danger.

Although people believe that vegetarians are quite limited when it comes to proteins, I want to break that myth and offer you a list of vegetarian protein sources.

The following list is a vegetarian protein that will help you lose weight:

- *Quinoa*
- *Greek yogurt*
- *Chickpeas*
- *Beans*
- *Lentils*
- *Seitan*
- *Peas*
- *Nutritional yeast*
- *Tofu*
- *Tempeh*

Next on the list of healthy ingredients that will help you slim, are the carbohydrates. There are many myths about carbohydrates – that they are not healthy, that they will make you fat, that you should completely cut them out of your meals.

The truth is somewhere in between. Eating only carbohydrates will undoubtedly lead to gaining extra weight. This is because the body will turn the carbs into glucose, which is the main brain's fuel. When the brain has the energy that comes from carbs, it will not bother about other sources for energy. Therefore, the fat that you consumed will be stored around your stomach, arms, back, and legs. This is because the fat is the second-best option for energy for the body, and when it is not using it, it stores it for "rainy days."

You are allowed to eat carbohydrates, as long as you have a healthy amount of proteins and fat on your plate. The rule 40-30-30 should be applied – 40 percent of carbs, 30 percent of fats, and 30 percent of proteins.

Only then you will provide your body with enough of everything, so it will not have to store the fats. Everything will be used (carbs as fuel and the fats will be burned).

The following list contains carbohydrates that are excellent for weight loss:

- *Spinach*
- *Bananas*
- *Apples*
- *Carrots*
- *Wholegrain bread*
- *Wholegrain pasta*
- *Rice*
- *Mango*

Just like carbs, fats also have a bad reputation, because people believe that fats make them fat. Only when the amount of carbs is drastically more extensive than the number of fats you consume, you will gain the unattractive fat layers.

When you restrict the number of carbs, and when the body needs additional sources for energy, it will turn to the fats you ate and will burn them at the same time.

This is the list with healthy fats that you should include on your vegetarian menu:

- *Cheese*
- *Avocado*
- *Extra virgin olive oil*
- *Nuts*
- *Seeds*
- *Olive*
- *Flaxseed (ground or oil)*

Finally, your fiber is as important as any other nutrient. Fiber helps our stomach digest the food quickly and without issues.

Fiber is found in fruits, veggies, beans, grains, and legumes. It is considered a type of carbohydrate that is excellent for your digestion.

There are three types of fiber, and they have various functions and multiple health benefits:

Soluble fiber – It helps in slowing the emptying process in the stomach, or in simpler words, it will keep you full for a longer time. Soluble fiber helps in lowering cholesterol and balances blood glucose levels. It is found in fruits, vegetables, barley, legumes, and oats.

Insoluble fiber – This fiber absorbs water, which helps to soften the contents of our bowels; it also supports regular bowel movements. Insoluble fiber also helps you feel full for a longer time and keeps the bowel environment healthy. It is found in wholegrain breads and cereals, seeds, nuts, wheat bran, and in the skin of fruit and vegetables (this is why you always hear that you should not peel some fruits off such as apples).

Resistant starch – This type of fiber cannot be digested in the small intestine; it proceeds to the large intestine where it can help in the production of good bacteria that betters the bowel health. Resistant starch is in ripe bananas, rice (cooked or cooled), undercooked pasta.

An adult man needs thirty grams of fibers per day, while adult women need twenty-five grams per day, for proper and healthy functioning.

- *Avoid saturated oils and spreads.* I know how delicious saturated oils and spreads are, but they will not help you maintain a slender figure in the long run. Instead, substitute them with unsaturated fats.

- *Unsaturated fats such as olive and sunflower oils and vegetables* are a healthy option than butter, ghee, or other fats. You do not have to avoid them entirely since fat gives energy, but as a beginner, you can limit the intake.

- *Cut down foods that are packed in salt and sugar.* Chocolate, chips, pastries, cakes, cookies, puddings, and other delicious junk food is not a healthy option even if they are entirely vegetarian. Foods that contain a large amount of sugar or salt than the daily recommendation may create health issues such as diabetes, high blood pressure, skin issues, cellulite. Start the transition slowly – whenever you feel like eating something sweet, reach for a banana or an apple. If that bag of chips is teasing you to open it, instead take a handful of nuts or at least popcorn that does not contain a large amount of salt (or butter or other additives).

- Finally, *fruits and vegetables* are your first choice in this diet. Use the abundance of these foods. Supermarkets and farmer's markets offer all kinds of fruits and veggies all year round. They are packed in vitamins and minerals and will satisfy your hunger and boost your body with the needed nutrients for the day.

Keeping your weight balanced during pregnancy

Some women decide to continue their vegetarian diet during pregnancy. It is essential to get enough vitamins and minerals so the fetus will develop properly. The same goes for once you deliver your child and start breastfeeding.

If you decide to raise your child on the vegetarian diet, make sure he or she consumes a wide variety of vegetarian foods that will provide enough vitamins, minerals, iron, proteins, fiber, and fat.

VEGETARIAN FOODS THAT WILL HELP YOU LOSE WEIGHT

Protein is a crucial nutrient that your body needs, especially when you are trying to slim. It helps in speeding the metabolism, suppresses hunger, and affects the change of several hormones that regulate weight loss.

A high protein intake speeds the metabolism because of its high thermic effect and other factors that assist in the burn of calories. Proteins reduce cravings, which is the thing you want while trying to cut down some weight; if you consume them in sufficient amounts, especially during breakfast, you will not feel the need to eat in between meals throughout the day.

Sources of protein

While for meat-eaters, proteins are easily found in meat (and meat and dairy products), vegetarians have to focus on plant-based foods that are rich in proteins.

But now, it is important to consume protein-rich foods that will be both vegetarian and will help you lose extra weight.

Here are some vegetarian protein-rich foods that are excellent for weight loss

Lentils (dal) – A cup of cooked lentils contains 18 grams of protein; you can cook it and make a soup, use it in your salads, or as a side in your main meal dish. Lentils are packed in carbs that are digested slowly, which means it also has fiber (excellent for good digestion and weight loss). The fact that it is rich in iron, manganese, and folate, makes it an even more valuable food for vegetarians.

Chickpeas (Chana) – Chickpeas are classified as legumes, and are a rich source of proteins. A cup of cooked chickpeas has about fifteen grams of proteins. Besides that, it is a wonderful source of complex carbs, folate, fiber, phosphorus, manganese, potassium, and iron.

Quinoa and amaranth – Excellent source of proteins that are gluten-free; both grains will keep you full for a longer time and will not cause you any cravings in between meals. The great thing is that you can combine them with both sweet and salty foods.

Spinach – This leafy green has more proteins than a hard-boiled egg and even half calories less. Sounds excellent if you are a vegetarian who wants to lose weight while providing your body with healthy nutrients.

Almonds – A few almonds a day will help you slim efficiently; it's a good base in the morning before your breakfast, or a healthy snack that will satisfy your hunger between meals.

Cottage Cheese – packed in protein, but also in calcium, vitamin B12, riboflavin, phosphorus, and other nutrients excellent for a healthy slimming.

Broccoli – Although many people are not a fan of it, broccoli is a rich source of vitamins C and K and fiber. It is a healthy and high-protein vegetable that will keep you full and will help your digestion.

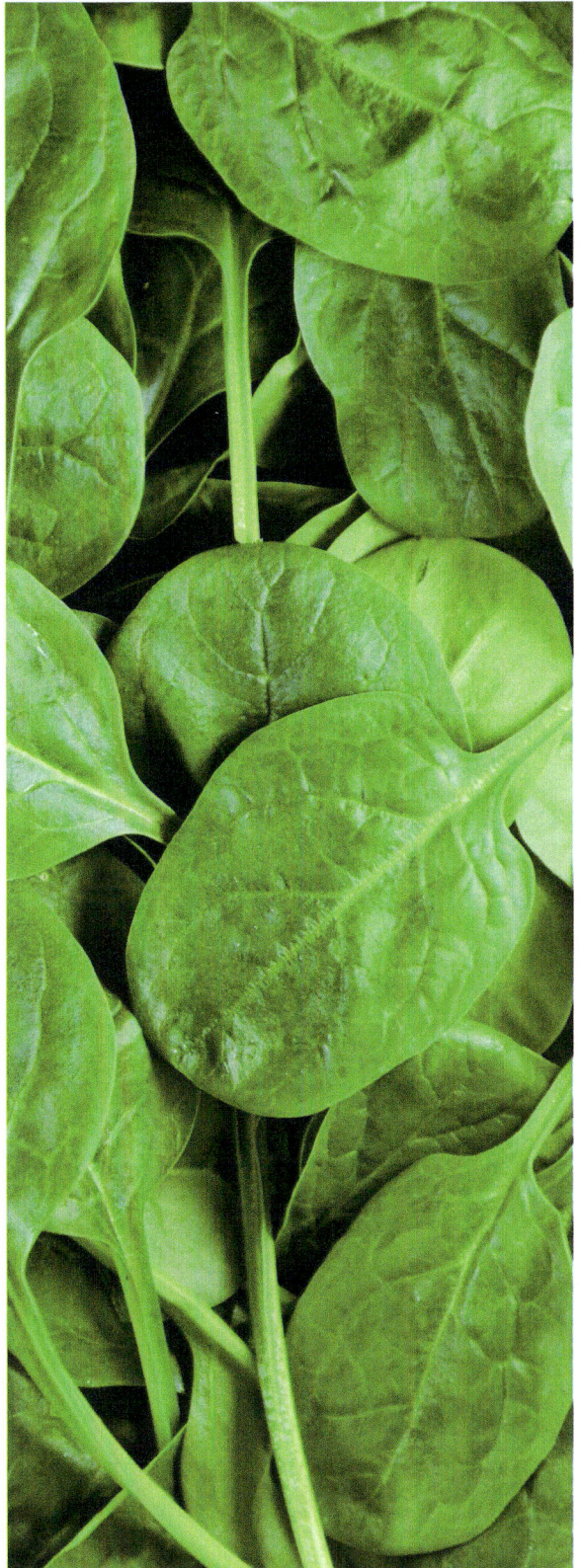

COMBINE VEGETARIAN DIET WITH INTERMITTENT FASTING

Intermittent fasting is one of the ideal ways to lose weight effectively. The thing with intermittent fasting is that you can eat your meals regularly within your regular time (this time is called fed state), and once those hours are over, you will no longer eat.

This way, you limit your calorie intake, while your body digests the food you ate during the day.

You can pick one of the methods (10 hours of fed state and 14 hours of fasting; 12 hours reserved for eating your meals and 12 hours for fasting; 8:16, 6:18).

People fear that they will crave foods once the fed state is over, but once you create this habit and remain disciplined, you will no longer feel the need to munch snacks in the middle of the night.

If you are a beginner, you can try it out a few times a week and see how it will work for you.

Some people practice intermittent fasting (no matter what diet they follow) constantly, every day.

Finally, you can fast even when you don't feel hunger and choose to skip a meal. People often eat in regular hours even when they are not hungry. This is a habit that provides your body with extra food, while the previous meal is not properly digested.

Next time you have a heavy breakfast, you do not have to have your lunch a few hours later only because it is a habit you have been practicing your entire life.

But, there are some more challenging methods such as fasting that can last for two days; these methods allow you to eat regularly your meals for five days, and then for two days, you do not eat anything. If it is too challenging, you can consume only 700 calories (mainly soups or liquid food). However, do not jump in this method before preparing your body and mind; start with the easier methods and see how you will react. Going two days without food can only cause you health issues (fatigue, headaches, irritability, and sickness).

34

What can you drink while fasting?

During the fasting hours, you are allowed to drink water (although some people are rigorous and don't drink water when they fast).
Since you are a beginner, you can surely drink water. Also, any drink that does not contain sugars (black coffee or tea) is a good option.
Once you start fasting, stay away from sweetened drinks (soda, soft drinks) and alcohol (it is rich in sugars that will not work well with your fasting).

How to start fasting on the vegetarian diet

The good thing about mixing both intermittent fasting and vegetarianism is that there is not a special rule about it. The only thing you need to follow is the method that suits you the best.
Create your fasting hours and simply follow your vegetarian weight loss menu. There is no need to rush into it and stress your body. Start slowly and see how you react to the fasting hours. Usually, people can endure longer ratios (8:16, 10:14, 12:12) without any problems. All they have to do is resist the urge to snack in between meals once the fasting starts.
However, don't jump into the challenging methods such as the 5:2, or the so-called Warrior diet (4 hours of eating and 20 hours of fasting). It can be quite a shock; if you are a woman, stick to the longer daily ratios rather than going for the harsh ones (long fasting can affect the hormones that affect your menstrual cycle).
If you want to give intermittent fasting a chance, create a meal plan that will have plenty of healthy vegetarian foods, mainly the ones that will keep you full for a long time.
See it as a goal you need to accomplish within a few weeks or a few months. After your scheduled time for weight loss passes and you see the desired results, then intermittent fasting is a successful tool for you. But, if things don't work out for you, it does not mean you failed; it simply means that intermittent fasting is not the ideal eating plan for you.

Is intermittent fasting safe long term?

Intermittent fasting is entirely safe in the long run if we assume you stick to the method that is not harming your health (10:12, 8:16, 12:12).

Occasionally, you can go with the more challenging methods, but as long as you do not do them frequently (not more than once a week), you are entirely safe to do it as well.

However, the best way to know this is to take a blood sample test and do a routine check; if there is some health problem, your doctor will recommend to stay away from fasting for as long as it needed.

When it comes to the side effects of fasting, there is naturally the hunger it occurs at the beginning. You might feel tired or irritable, but these symptoms are normal because your body sees this fasting state as hunger and is warning you to provide the system with food.

Intermittent fasting is the test of your character; if you managed to pass it, you would be able to do it without problems (of course, if we assume you are entirely healthy).

What you must not forget is to stay hydrated; water will help your digestion, but also it will suppress your cravings in between meals.

And finally, if you wonder if fasting while following the vegetarian diet is worth it, just keep in mind that fasting works with any diet (meat, plant-based, keto, paleo, and so on).

It is a healthy way to lose weight while still eating every meal of the day during your active hours. With fasting, you allow your body to rest from extra food and extra work that it does to digest the food while you sleep.

While in the fasting state, your body gains energy from the stored fats by burning them, and this is how you slim.

The initial results will be visible within a week.

AIR FRYER AND HOW IT WORKS?

The technology used in air fryers is called "Rapid Air Technology" which causes the heat to be pushed by a rapidly turning fan. Ovens, unless they are convection style, do not have fans that constantly circulate the heat. Air fryers have a removable basket in which the food sits, and the hot air circulates all around to cook the food.

One of the most popular things to make in an air fryer is French fries. These tasty treats are normally submerged in a vat full of oil and are dep fried at high heat. The potatoes soak up quite a bit of the oil and retain it, and it is consumed. We all know that oil is not necessarily good for the body. Some oils cause plaque to form in our blood vessels and encumber our bodies with extra fat. If you reduce the amount of oil and the food tastes great, how can you go wrong?

Is Food Really Healthier When Made In An Air Fryer?

The fan in the air fryer not only circulates hot air around the food, but it also circulates out droplets of oil and creates a chemical reaction called The Mallard Effect. This effect causes the food to turn brown and crispy and adds some flavor to the food. Air fried foods contain much less fat, but they taste is about the same, and sometimes even better. Not only do foods contain less fat, but they also have fewer calories. When food is fried, a compound is created on the food that we consume. This substance is acrylamide, and it is thought to be a carcinogen (cancer-causing).

A study was performed, and it was found that the acrylamide content was reduced by 90% when food was cooked in an air fryer.

Benefits

Food is healthier because oil use is greatly reduced. Still, everything comes out crispy and brown that is supposed to.

Food cooks quicker and more efficently. Heat does not escape from the air fryer like it does on a cooktop or oven. It takes less time to cook or reheat food because it stays in the air fryer and circulates.

The air fryer is more efficient. Because the heat stays in the unit and does not vent, it cooks more efficiently and faster without using as much electricity. I hate turning my oven on in the summer because it heats up the house.

Not so with an air fryer. the heat created in the air fryer stays in the air fryer.

It is versatile, and you can make a variety of foods ranging from breakfast items to mouth-watering desserts.

Most units are small and fit on the counter top or in a cupboard for storage

They are quite easy to clean, with lots of detahcable parts and components that can be placed in the dish washer.

Heating up frozen foods that would normally go in an oven at high temperature can be cooked in a matter of minutes.

Accessories

Some air fryers come with accessories, and they include:

- Racks that go inside the basket
- Grill pan
- Baking dish
- Steamer
- Silicone pan or cups
- Rubber ended tongs that do not scratch

It is worth getting the silicone pan or cups, steamer and baking dish, and absolutely necessary to get rubber ended tongs.

Don't try removing food from the basket with a fork because you will scratch the surface of the basket and everything will stick in the future.

The 6-inch basket fits perfectly into the air fryer with a little room to fit the rubber tipped tongs in to get it out. The 4-inch basket is perfect for making single serve omelets, or you can use a ramekin.

BREAKFAST RECIPES

EXQUISITE DUTCH PANCAKE

Cooking Difficulty: 2/10	Cooking Time: 15 minutes	Servings: 4

INGREDIENTS

- 3 eggs, beaten
- 2 tbsps. vegan butter
- ½ c. flour
- 2 tbsps. powdered sugar
- ½ c. coconut milk
- 1½ c. freshly sliced strawberries

STEP 1
Preheat your Air Fryer to 330 degrees F.

STEP 2
Set a pan on low heat and melt butter. In a medium-sized bowl, mix flour, milk, eggs, and vanilla until fully incorporated. Add the mixture to the pan with melted butter.

STEP 3
Place the pan in your air fryer's cooking basket and bake for 12-16 minutes until the pancake is fluffy and golden brown.

STEP 4
Drizzle powdered sugar and toss sliced strawberries on top. Serve and enjoy!

NUTRITIONAL INFORMATION
Calories: 196, Fat: 9g, Carbs: 19g, Protein: 16g

BAKED CAULIFLOWER WITH CHEESE

Cooking Difficulty: 3/10	Cooking Time: 26 minutes	Servings: 4

NUTRITIONAL INFORMATION
Calories: 239, Fat: 12.2g, Carbs: 16.1g, Protein: 16g

INGREDIENTS

- 2 tbsps. vegan butter
- 4 c. cauliflower florets
- 1 c. oat milk
- 2/3 c. cooked quinoa
- ¼ c. parsley
- 4 oz. mozzarella cheese, grated
- sea salt
- freshly ground black pepper

STEP 1

Preheat your Air Fryer to 360°F.

STEP 2

In a saucepan, boil water. Add cauliflower florets and then cook for 1 minute. Drain and set aside.

STEP 3

In a mixing bowl, place cauliflower florets and then add butter, milk, quinoa, and parsley. Season with salt and pepper to taste. Mix well together.

STEP 4

Transfer mixture into a casserole dish that can fit into the size of the Air Fryer cooking basket, cook in batches if needed. Sprinkle with mozzarella cheese.

STEP 5

Place casserole dish in Air Fryer cooking basket.

STEP 6

Cook for about 20-25 minutes, or until cooked through and cheese is melted. Serve and enjoy!

CRAVING CINNAMON TOAST

Cooking Difficulty: 1/10	Cooking Time: 6 minutes	Servings: 6

INGREDIENTS

- 12 slices bread
- pepper
- ½ c. sugar
- vegan butter
- 1½ tsps. vanilla extract
- 1½ tsps. cinnamon

STEP 1
Preheat your Air Fryer up to 400 degrees F.

STEP 2
In a microwave-proof bowl, mix butter, pepper, sugar, and vanilla extract. Warm the mixture for 30 seconds until everything melts as you stir.

STEP 3
Pour the mixture over bread slices. Lay the bread slices in your air fryer's cooking basket and cook for 5 minutes.

STEP 4
Serve with fresh banana and berry sauce. Enjoy!

NUTRITIONAL INFORMATION
Calories: 217, Fat: 12.5g, Carbs: 4.7g, Protein: 18.8g

BLUEBERRY CREAM CHEESE WITH FRENCH TOAST

Cooking Difficulty: 2/10	Cooking Time: 10 minutes	Servings: 4

NUTRITIONAL INFORMATION
Calories: 428, Fat: 11.3g, Carbs: 53.7g, Protein: 23.4g

INGREDIENTS

- 2 eggs, beaten
- 4 slices bread
- 3 tsps. sugar
- 1½ c. corn flakes
- 1/3 c. vegan milk
- ¼ tsp. nutmeg
- 4 tbsps. berry-flavored cheese
- ¼ tsp. salt

STEP 1
Preheat your Air Fryer to 400 degrees F.

STEP 2
In a medium bowl, mix sugar, eggs, nutmeg, salt, and milk.

STEP 3
In a separate bowl, mix blueberries and cheese.

STEP 4
Take 2 bread slices and gently pour the blueberry mixture over the slices. Top with the milk mixture.

STEP 5
Cover with the remaining two slices to make sandwiches. Dredge the sandwiches over cornflakes to coat well.

STEP 6
Lay the sandwiches in your air fryer's cooking basket and cook for 8 minutes.

STEP 7
Serve with berries and syrup. Enjoy!

AVOCADO MUFFINS

	Cooking Difficulty: 3/10		Cooking Time: 12 minutes		Servings: 7

INGREDIENTS

- 1 c. almond flour
- ½ tsp. baking soda
- 1 tsp. apple cider vinegar
- 1 oz. melted dark chocolate
- 1 egg
- 4 tbsps. vegan butter
- 3 scoops stevia powder
- ½ c. pitted avocado

STEP 1
Preheat the Air Fryer to 355°F. Whisk the almond flour, baking soda, and vinegar. Add the stevia powder and melted chocolate.

STEP 2
Whisk the egg in another container and add to the mixture along with the butter. Peel, cube, and mash the avocado and add. Blend with a hand mixer to make the flour mixture smooth. Pour into the muffin forms (½ full). Cook for 9 minutes.

STEP 3
Lower the heat (340°F) and cook for 3 more minutes. Chill before serving for the best results.

NUTRITIONAL INFORMATION
Calories: 133, Fat: 12.4g, Protein: 2.2g, Carbs: 2.9g

FETA BREAKFAST

Cooking Difficulty: 2/10	Cooking Time: 4 minutes	Servings: 2

NUTRITIONAL INFORMATION
Calories: 426, Fat: 14g, Carbs: 65g, Protein: 9g

INGREDIENTS

- 3½ lbs. feta cheese
- pepper
- 1 whole chopped onion
- 2 tbsps. chopped parsley
- 1 egg yolk
- olive oil
- 5 sheets frozen filo pastry

STEP 1
Preheat your Air Fryer to 400 degrees F.

STEP 2
Cut each of the 5 filo sheets into three equal sized strips.

STEP 3
Cover the strips with olive oil.

STEP 4
In a bowl, mix onion, pepper, feta, salt, egg yolk, and parsley.

STEP 5
Make triangles using the cut strips and add a little bit of the feta mixture on top of each triangle.

STEP 6
Place the triangles in your air fryer's cooking basket and cook for 3 minutes.

STEP 7
Serve alongside green onions and a drizzle of olive oil.

STEP 8
Enjoy!

AVOCADO EGG

Cooking Difficulty: 2/10	Cooking Time: 7 minutes	Servings: 4

INGREDIENTS

- 2 avocado
- 4 eggs
- chopped chives
- chopped parsley
- pepper

STEP 1
Warm up the fryer to 350ºF.

STEP 2
Remove the pit from the avocado. Slice and scoop out part of the flesh. Shake with the seasonings.

STEP 3
Add an egg to each half and place in the preheated Air Fryer for 6 minutes.

STEP 4
Remove and serve with some additional parsley and chives if desired.

NUTRITIONAL INFORMATION
Calories: 288, Fat: 26g, Protein: 7.6g, Carbs: 9.4 g

POTATO PANCAKES

Cooking Difficulty: 3/10	Cooking Time: 10 minutes	Servings: 4

NUTRITIONAL INFORMATION
Calories: 255, Fat: 8.4 g, Carbs: 42 g, Protein: 7.1 g

INGREDIENTS

- 200g potatoes, cleaned and peeled
- 1 chopped onion
- 1 egg, beaten
- ¼ c. oat milk
- ½ tsp. garlic powder
- ¼ tsp. kosher salt
- 3 tbsps. all-purpose flour
- ground black pepper

STEP 1
Shred the peeled potatoes and then transfer in a bowl filled with cold water to wash off excess starch.

STEP 2
Drain the potatoes and the use of paper towels to dry off the potatoes.

STEP 3
In a mixing bowl, combine together egg, garlic powder, salt and pepper, and lastly the flour. Stir well. Add in shredded potatoes.

STEP 4
Preheat Air Fryer to 390°F.

STEP 5
Pull out the Air Fryer cooking basket and then place ¼ cup of the potato pancake batter in the cooking basket.

STEP 6
Cook until golden brown for approximately 10 minutes.

STEP 7
Serve and enjoy!

CINNAMON FLAVORED GRILLED PINEAPPLES

Cooking Difficulty: 3/10	Cooking Time: 20 minutes	Servings: 4

INGREDIENTS

- 1 tsp. cinnamon
- 5 pineapple slices
- ½ c. brown sugar
- 1 tbsp. chopped basil
- 1 tbsp. honey

STEP 1
Preheat your air fryer to 340 degrees F. Using a bowl, combine cinnamon and brown sugar.

STEP 2
Drizzle the sugar mixture over your pineapple slices and set aside for about 20 minutes.

STEP 3
Place the pineapple rings in the air fryer cooking basket and cook for 10 minutes. Flip the pineapples and cook for 10 minutes more. Serve with basil and a drizzle of honey.

NUTRITIONAL INFORMATION
Calories: 480, Fat: 18g, Carbs: 71g, Protein: 13g

HERBED SWEET POTATO HASH

| Cooking Difficulty: 3/10 | Cooking Time: 20 minutes | Servings: 5 |

INGREDIENTS

- 4 sweet potatoes, peeled and diced
- 1 c. sliced button mushrooms
- 1 chopped onion
- ½ chopped green bell pepper
- 2 tbsps. lemon juice
- 2 tbsps. olive oil
- ½ tsp. thyme, dried
- ½ tsp. rosemary, dried
- salt, and pepper

STEP 1
Preheat Air Fryer to 360°F.

STEP 2
In a mixing bowl, mix together all ingredients. Season with salt and pepper.

STEP 3
Take out Air Fryer cooking basket, and then place sweet potato mixture.

STEP 4
Cook for about 25-30 minutes.

STEP 5
Serve and enjoy!

NUTRITIONAL INFORMATION
Calories: 203, Fat: 6.5g, Carbs: 36.2g, Protein: 3.4g

SPINACH FRITTATA WITH CHERRY TOMATO

Cooking Difficulty: 2/10	Cooking Time: 15 minutes	Servings: 4

NUTRITIONAL INFORMATION
Calories: 215, Fat: 12.9g, Carbs: 8.5g, Protein: 14.2g

INGREDIENTS

- 6 eggs
- kosher salt
- ground black pepper
- 2 tbsps. olive oil
- 1 chopped onion
- 1 c. halved cherry tomatoes
- 8 oz. spinach leaves
- 3 oz. grated cheddar (optional)

STEP 1
Preheat oven to 390°F.

STEP 2
In a mixing bowl, whisk 6 eggs together a season with salt and pepper to taste. Set aside.

STEP 3
Set a skillet over medium high heat and heat olive oil. Stir-fry the onion for 3 minutes, then add the spinach leaves and cherry tomatoes. Cook for 3 minutes, stirring often.

STEP 4
Transfer vegetables in a small baking pan (enough to fit Air Fryer), pour the beaten eggs. Sprinkle with cheddar cheese.

STEP 5
Place baking pan in the Air Fryer cooking basket and cook for about 10 minutes.

STEP 6
Serve and enjoy!

ZUCCHINI EGG NESTS

Cooking Difficulty: 2/10	Cooking Time: 10 minutes	Servings: 5

INGREDIENTS

- 10 oz. grated zucchini
- olive oil
- ¼ tsp. sea salt
- ¼ tsp onion powder
- ½ tsp. black pepper
- ½ tsp. paprika
- 5 eggs
- 5 oz. shredded cheddar cheese (optional)
- 5 ramekins

STEP 1
Preheat the Air Fryer at 356ºF.

STEP 2
Grate the zucchini. Add olive oil to the ramekins and add the zucchini in a nest shape. Sprinkle with the paprika, onion powder, salt, and pepper.

STEP 3
Whisk the eggs and add to the nest, topping it off with the cheese.

STEP 4
Air fry for 7 minutes. Chill for 3 minutes and serve in the ramekin.

NUTRITIONAL INFORMATION
Calories: 221, Fat: 17.7g, Protein: 13.4g, Carbs: 2.9g

MUSHROOM OMELETTE

Cooking Difficulty: 2/10	Cooking Time: 15 minutes	Servings: 5

INGREDIENTS

- 1 tbsp. olive oil
- 2 c. sliced mushrooms
- 1 small sliced onion
- 2 eggs
- ½ c. grated cheese (optional)
- parsley

STEP 1
Program the Air Fryer to 320ºF.

STEP 2
Warm up a skillet (medium heat) and add the oil.

STEP 3
Toss in the mushrooms, parsley, and onions and sauté for about 5 minutes. Add to the Air Fryer.

STEP 4
Whisk the eggs and dump on top of the fixings in the fryer.

STEP 5
Sprinkle with the cheese and air fry for 10 minutes. Take right out of the basket and serve.

NUTRITIONAL INFORMATION
Calories: 221, Fat: 17.7g, Protein: 13.4g, Carbs: 2.9g

DESERVING CHEESY OMELETTE

	Cooking Difficulty: 2/10		Cooking Time: 15 minutes		Servings: 1

NUTRITIONAL INFORMATION
Calories: 396, Fat: 32g, Carbs: 1g, Protein: 27g

INGREDIENTS

- 2 eggs, beaten
- pepper
- 1 c. shredded cheddar cheese (optional)
- 1 chopped onion
- 2 tbsps. soy sauce

STEP 1

Preheat your Air Fryer up to 340 degrees F.

STEP 2

Drizzle soy sauce over the chopped onions.

STEP 3

Place the onions in your air fryer's cooking basket and cook for 8 minutes.

STEP 4

In a medium bowl, mix the beaten eggs with salt and pepper.

STEP 5

Pour the egg mixture over onions (in the cooking basket) and cook for 3 minutes.

STEP 6

Add cheddar cheese over eggs and bake for 2 more minutes.

STEP 7

Serve with fresh basil and enjoy!

THE GREAT JAPANESE OMELETTE

Cooking Difficulty: 2/10	Cooking Time: 13 minutes	Servings: 1

INGREDIENTS

- 1 cubed japanese tofu
- 3 whole eggs
- pepper
- 1 tsp. coriander
- 1 tsp. cumin
- 2 tbsps. soy sauce
- 2 tbsps. chopped green onion
- olive oil
- 1 chopped onion
- 1 tomato (optional)

STEP 1
Preheat your Air Fryer up to 400 degrees F.

STEP 2
Using a medium bowl, mix eggs, soy sauce, pepper, oil, and salt.

STEP 3
Add cubed tofu to baking forms and pour the egg mixture on top. Place the prepared forms in the air fryer cooking basket and cook for 10 minutes.

STEP 5
Serve with a sprinkle of herbs. Enjoy!

NUTRITIONAL INFORMATION
Calories: 300, Fat: 40g, Carbs: 19g, Protein: 72g

AIR FRIED HASHBROWN

Cooking Difficulty: 3/10	Cooking Time: 20 minutes	Servings: 4

NUTRITIONAL INFORMATION
Calories: 207, Fat: 9.3 g, Carbs: 30.1 g, Protein - 3.2 g

INGREDIENTS

- 4 (200g) potatoes, cleaned and peeled
- 3 tbsps. butter, melted
- ½ tsp. cayenne pepper
- ½ tsp. ground cumin
- salt and black pepper

STEP 1

Shred peeled potatoes and then drench in cold water. Stir the potatoes and let it soak until water is translucent – these are the starch from the potatoes. Drain water and then pour another batch of cold water. Repeat the Directions: again.

STEP 2

Transfer the potatoes in a flat tray and then pat dry using paper towels. Preheat your Air Fryer to 390°F.

STEP 3

In a mixing bowl, combine together butter, cayenne pepper, cumin, salt, and black pepper. Add in the shredded potatoes and stir together.

STEP 4

Take out the Air Fryer cooking basket. Scoop about 2 Tbsp. of the potato mixture and then mold it to the desired shape. Place in the cooking basket.

STEP 5

Cook hash brown until golden brown for 15 minutes. Serve and enjoy!

MAIN RECIPES

CHILI ROASTED EGGPLANT SOBA

 Cooking Difficulty: 3/10	 Cooking Time: 19 minutes	 Servings: 4

INGREDIENTS

- 200g eggplants
- kosher salt
- ground black pepper

noodles:

- 8 oz. soba noodles
- 1 c. sliced button mushrooms
- 2 tbsps. peanut oil
- 2 tbsps. light soy sauce
- 1 tbsp. rice vinegar
- 2 tbsps. chopped cilantro
- 2 chopped red chili pepper
- 1 tsp. sesame oil

NUTRITIONAL INFORMATION
Calories: 318, Fat: 8.2g, Carbs: 54g, Protein: 11.3g

STEP 1

In a mixing bowl, mix together ingredients for the marinade.

STEP 2

Wash eggplants and then slice into ¼-inch thick cuts. Season with salt and pepper, to taste.

STEP 3

Preheat your Air Fryer to 390°F.

STEP 4

Place eggplants in the Air Fryer cooking basket. Cook for 10 minutes.

STEP 5

Meanwhile, cook the soba noodles according to packaging directions. Drain the noodles.

STEP 6

In a large mixing bowl, combine the peanut oil, soy sauce, rice vinegar, cilantro, chili, and sesame oil. Mix well.

STEP 7

Add the cooked soba noodles, mushrooms, and roasted eggplants; toss to coat.

STEP 8

Transfer mixture into the Air Fryer cooking basket. Cook for another 5 minutes.

STEP 9

Serve and enjoy!

MARINATED PORTABELLO MUSHROOM

Cooking Difficulty: 2/10	Cooking Time: 20 minutes	Servings: 4

NUTRITIONAL INFORMATION
Calories: 96, Fat: 7.9g, Carbs: 7.5g, Protein: 3.6g

INGREDIENTS

- 4 pcs. portabello mushrooms
- 1 chopped shallot
- 1 tsp. minced garlic
- 2 tbsps. olive oil
- 2 tbsps. balsamic vinegar
- ground black pepper

STEP 1

Clean and wash portabello mushrooms and remove stems. Set aside.

STEP 2

In a bowl, mix together the shallot, garlic, olive oil, and balsamic vinegar. Season with pepper, to taste.

STEP 3

Arrange portabello mushrooms, cap side up and brush with balsamic vinegar mixture. Let it stand for at least 30 minutes.

STEP 4

Preheat your Air Fryer to 360°F.

STEP 5

Place marinated portabello mushroom on Air Fryer cooking basket. Cook for about 15-20 minutes or until mushrooms are tender.

STEP 6

Serve and enjoy!

BAKED GARLIC PARSLEY POTATOES

	Cooking Difficulty: 3/10		Cooking Time: 38 minutes		Servings: 4

NUTRITIONAL INFORMATION

Calories: 147, Fat: 3.7g, Carbs: 26.7g, Protein: 3g

INGREDIENTS

- 3 russet potatoes
- 2 tbsps. olive oil
- 1 tbsp. salt
- 1 tbsp. garlic powder
- 1 tsp. parsley

STEP 1

Rinse the potatoes under running water and pierce with a fork in several places.

STEP 2

Season with salt and garlic and drizzle with olive oil. Rub the seasonings with your hands, so the potatoes are evenly coated.

STEP 3

Put the potatoes in the basket of your air fryer and slide it into the air fryer.

STEP 4

Set the temperature of 400 °F and the timer for 35 minutes and turn the button On Check the doneness and once the potatoes are fork tender remove from the fryer.

STEP 5

Serve the potatoes garnished with chopped fresh parsley and topped with a dollop of sour cream.

FRIED GREEN BEANS GARLIC

Cooking Difficulty: 2/10	Cooking Time: 5 minutes	Servings: 2

INGREDIENTS

- ¾ c. chopped green beans
- 2 tsps. granulated garlic
- 2 tbsps. rosemary
- ½ tsp. salt
- olive oil

STEP 1
Preheat an Air Fryer to 390°F (200°C).

STEP 2
Place the chopped green beans in the Air Fryer then brush with olive oil.

STEP 3
Sprinkle salt, garlic, and rosemary over the green beans, then cook for 5 minutes.

STEP 4
Once the green beans are done, remove from the Air Fryer then place on a serving dish.

STEP 5
Serve and enjoy warm.

NUTRITIONAL INFORMATION
Calories: 72, Fat: 6.3g, Protein: 0.7g, Carbs: 4.5g

ZUCCHINI, TOMATO AND MOZZARELLA PIE

Cooking Difficulty: 3/10	Cooking Time: 25 minutes	Servings: 4

INGREDIENTS

- 3 medium zucchinis
- sea salt
- 5 minced cloves garlic
- freshly ground pepper
- olive oil
- 8 oz. sliced mozzarella
- 3 sliced vine-ripe or heirloom tomatoes
- freshly chopped basil

NUTRITIONAL INFORMATION
Calories: 195, Fat: 10.4g, Carbs: 9.6g, Protein: 18.2g

STEP 1
Preheat the air fryer to 400 °F.

STEP 2
Halve the zucchini and thinly cut lengthwise into strips

STEP 3
Apply pepper and salt for seasoning and allow to sit in a colander for 9-10 minutes.

STEP 4
Transfer to paper towels to drain.

STEP 5
In an even layer, arrange the zucchini in a small baking dish and sprinkle with the minced garlic and pepper.

STEP 6
Sprinkle with olive oil and top with the mozzarella slices, followed by the tomato slices.

STEP 7
Sprinkle with the chopped basil, sea salt, and pepper.

STEP 8
Place the pan in the basket and bake at 400 °F for 25 minutes, until the cheese has melted.

STEP 9
Remove from the air fryer and let it sit for 10 minutes.

STEP 10
Serve warm and enjoy.

CAULIFLOWER FLORETS IN TOMATO PUREE

Cooking Difficulty: 4/10	Cooking Time: 17 minutes	Servings: 2

INGREDIENTS

- 2 c. cauliflower florets
- 3 tsps. granulated garlic
- ½ tsp. salt
- ½ tsp. coriander
- 2 c. water
- 3 eggs
- ½ tsp. pepper
- ¼ c. grated mozzarella cheese
- 3 tbsps. tomato puree

NUTRITIONAL INFORMATION

Calories: 276, Fat: 21.8g, Protein: 13.8g, Carbs: 5.4g

STEP 1

Place garlic, salt, and coriander in a container then pour water into it. Stir until the seasoning is completely dissolved.

STEP 2

Add the cauliflower florets to the brine then submerge for at least 30 minutes.

STEP 3

After 30 minutes, remove the cauliflower florets from the brine, then wash and rinse them. Pat them dry.

STEP 4

Preheat an Air Fryer to 400°F (204°C). Crash the eggs and place in a bowl.

STEP 6

Season with pepper then whisks until incorporated.

STEP 7

Dip a cauliflower floret in the egg then place in the air fryer. Repeat with the remaining cauliflower florets and egg.

STEP 8

Cook the cauliflower florets for 12 minutes or until lightly golden and the egg is curly.

STEP 9

Drizzle tomato puree on top.

STEP 10

Cook the cauliflower florets again for another 5 minutes then remove from the Air Fryer. Transfer to a serving dish then serve. Enjoy warm.

AIR FRIED TOFU WITH PEANUT DIPPING SAUCE

Cooking Difficulty: 3/10	Cooking Time: 10 minutes	Servings: 6

NUTRITIONAL INFORMATION

Calories: 256, Fat: 14.1g, Carbs: 21.2g, Protein: 12.4 g.

INGREDIENTS

- 16 oz. cubed firm tofu
- 185g all-purpose flour
- ½ tsp. Himalayan salt
- ½ tsp. ground black pepper
- olive oil spray
  For the dipping sauce:
- 1/3 c. smooth low-sodium peanut butter
- 1 tsp. minced garlic
- 2 tbsps. light soy sauce
- 1 tbsp. fresh lime juice
- 1 tsp. brown sugar
- 1/3 c. water
- 2 tbsps. chopped roasted

STEP 1
In a bowl, mix all dipping sauce ingredients. Cover it with plastic wrap and keep refrigerated until ready to serve.

STEP 2
To make the fried tofu, season all-purpose flour with salt and pepper.

STEP 3
Coat the tofu cubes with the flour mixture. Spray with oil.

STEP 4
Preheat your Air Fryer to 390°F.

STEP 5
Place coated tofu in the cooking basket. Careful not to overcrowd them.

STEP 6
Cook until browned for approximately 8 minutes.

STEP 7
Serve with prepared peanut dipping sauce.

STEP 8
Enjoy!

SPAGHETTI WITH ROASTED VEGETABLES

Cooking Difficulty: 4/10	Cooking Time: 24 minutes	Servings: 4

INGREDIENTS

- 10 oz. spaghetti, cooked
- 1 eggplant, chopped
- 1 chopped bell pepper
- 1 zucchini, chopped
- 4 oz. halved grape tomatoes
- 1 tsp. minced garlic
- 4 tbsps. divided olive oil
- kosher salt
- ground black pepper
- 12 oz. can diced tomatoes
- ½ tsp. dried basil
- ½ tsp. dried oregano
- 1 tsp. Spanish paprika
- 1 tsp. brown sugar

NUTRITIONAL INFORMATION

Calories: 330, Fat: 12.4g, Carbs: 45.3g, Protein: 9.9g

STEP 1

In a mixing bowl, combine together eggplant, red bell pepper, zucchini, grape tomatoes, garlic, and 2 tablespoons olive oil. Add some salt and pepper, to taste.

STEP 2

Preheat your Air Fryer to 390°F.

STEP 3

Place vegetable mixture in the Air Fryer cooking basket and cook for about 10-12 minutes, or until vegetables are tender.

STEP 4

Meanwhile, you can start preparing the tomato sauce.

STEP 5

In a saucepan, heat remaining 2 tablespoons olive oil. Stir fry garlic for 2 minutes. Add diced tomatoes and simmer for 3 minutes.

STEP 6

Stir in basil, oregano, paprika, and brown sugar. Season with salt and pepper, to taste. Let it cook for another 5-7 minutes.

STEP 7

Once cooked, transfer the vegetables from Air Fryer to a mixing bowl.

STEP 8

Add the cooked spaghetti and prepared a sauce. Toss to combine well.

STEP 9

Divide among 4 serving plates. Serve and enjoy!

BROCCOLI POPCORN

 Cooking Difficulty: 2/10	 Cooking Time: 7 minutes	 Servings: 4

NUTRITIONAL INFORMATION
Calories: 202, Fat: 17.5g, Protein: 5.1g, Carbs: 7.8g

INGREDIENTS

- 2 c. broccoli florets
- 2 c. almond flour
- 4 egg yolks
- ½ tsp. salt
- ½ tsp. pepper

STEP 1

Soak the broccoli florets in salty water to remove all the insects inside.

STEP 2

Wash and rinse the broccoli florets then pat them dry.

STEP 3

Crack the eggs. Add almond flour to the liquid then season with salt and pepper. Mix until incorporated.

STEP 4

Preheat an Air Fryer to 375°F (191°C).Dip a broccoli floret in the coconut flour mixture then place in the Air Fryer. Repeat with the remaining broccoli florets.

STEP 5

Cook the broccoli florets 6 minutes. You may do this in several batches.

STEP 6

Once it is done, remove the fried broccoli popcorn from the Air Fryer then place on a serving dish.

STEP 7

Serve and enjoy immediately.

QUINOA AND SPINACH CAKES

Cooking Difficulty: 2/10	Cooking Time: 9 minutes	Servings: 10

INGREDIENTS

- 2 c. cooked quinoa
- 1 c. chopped baby spinach
- 1 egg
- 2 tbsps. minced parsley
- 1 tsp. minced garlic
- 1 carrot, peeled and shredded
- 1 chopped onion
- ¼ c. oat milk
- 1 c. breadcrumbs
- sea salt
- ground black peppe

STEP 1

In a mixing bowl, mix all ingredients. Season with salt and pepper to taste.

STEP 2

Preheat your Air Fryer to 390°F.

STEP 3

Scoop ¼ cup of quinoa and spinach mixture and place in the Air Fryer cooking basket. Cook in batches until browned for about 8 minutes.

STEP 4

Serve and enjoy!

NUTRITIONAL INFORMATION

Calories: 188, Fat: 4.4 g, Carbs: 31.2g, Protein: 8.1g

SPINACH IN CHEESE ENVELOPES

Cooking Difficulty: 3/10	Cooking Time: 15 minutes	Servings: 8

INGREDIENTS

- 1½ c. almond flour
- 3 egg yolks
- 2 eggs
- ½ c. cheddar cheese
- 2 c. steamed spinach
- ¼ tsp. salt
- ½ tsp. pepper
- 3 c. cream cheese
- ¼ c. chopped onion

NUTRITIONAL INFORMATION

Calories: 365, Fat: 34.6g, Protein: 10.4g, Carbs: 4.4g

STEP 1

Place cream cheese in a mixing bowl then whisks until soft and fluffy.

STEP 2

Add egg yolks to the mixing bowl then continue whisking until incorporated.

STEP 3

Stir in coconut flour to the cheese mixture then mix until becoming a soft dough.

STEP 4

Place the dough on a flat surface then roll until thin. Cut the thin dough into 8 squares then keep. Crash the eggs then place in a bowl.

STEP 5

Season with salt, pepper, and grated cheese, then mix well. Add chopped spinach and onion to the egg mixture, then stir until combined.

STEP 6

Put spinach filling on a square dough then fold until becoming an envelope. Repeat with the remaining spinach filling and dough. Glue with water.

STEP 7

Preheat an Air Fryer to 425°F (218°C).

STEP 8

Arrange the spinach envelopes in the Air Fryer then cook for 12 minutes or until lightly golden brown.

STEP 9

Remove from the Air Fryer then serve warm. Enjoy!

ZUCCHINI PARMESAN BITES

Cooking Difficulty: 3/10	Cooking Time: 12 minutes	Servings: 4

INGREDIENTS

- 4 medium zucchinis
- 1 c. grated coconuts
- 1-tbsp. Italian seasoning
- ¼ c. chopped parsley
- ½ c. grated parmesan cheese
- 1 egg

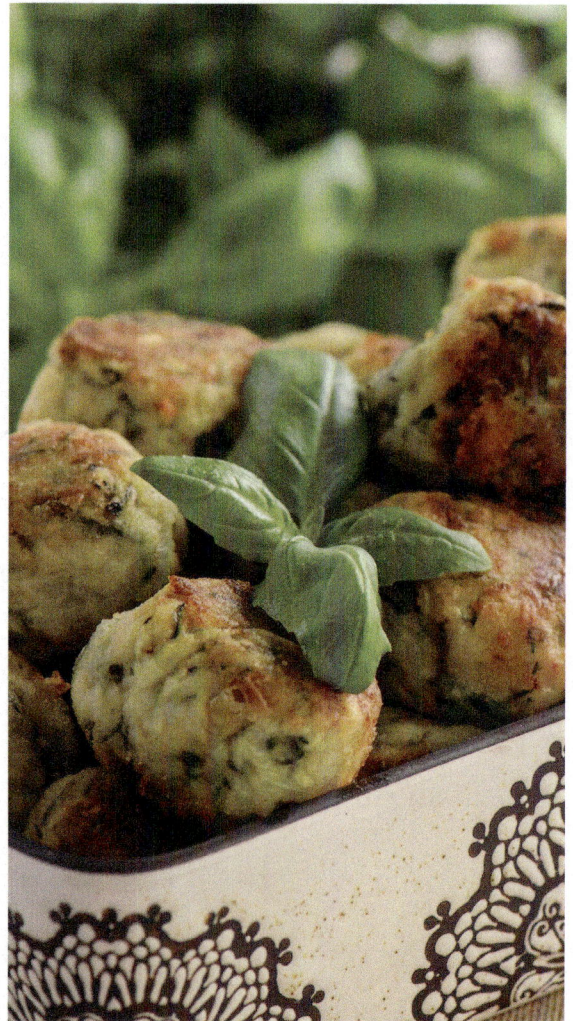

NUTRITIONAL INFORMATION
Calories: 225, Fat: 17.9g, Protein: 9g, Carbs: 10.6g

STEP 1
Peel the zucchinis then cut into halves.

STEP 2
Discard the seeds then grate the zucchinis. Place in a bowl.

STEP 3
Add grated coconuts, parsley, Italian seasoning, egg, and Parmesan cheese to the bowl. Mix well.

STEP 4
Shape the zucchini mixture into small balls forms then set aside.

STEP 5
Preheat an Air Fryer to 400°F (204°C).

STEP 6
Place a rack in the Air Fryer then arrange the zucchini balls on it.

STEP 7
Cook the zucchini balls for 10 minutes then remove from heat. Serve and enjoy.

PORTOBELLO PIZZA

Cooking Difficulty: 3/10	Cooking Time: 12 minutes	Servings: 3

NUTRITIONAL INFORMATION
Calories: 227, Fat: 17.1g, Carbs: 45g, Protein: 15.3g

INGREDIENTS

- 3 portobello mushrooms
- 3 tsps. pizza seasoning
- olive oil
- 3 slices tomato
- 1.5 oz. vegan mozzarella cheese
- 1.5 oz. monterey jack
- 12 pepperoni slices
- 1.5 oz. cheddar cheese

(optional)

STEP 1
Preheat the air fryer to 400 °F.

STEP 2
Rinse the mushrooms and remove the stems.

STEP 3
Arrange the mushrooms in the basket of your air fryer cap side down. Drizzle with little olive oil.

STEP 4
Sprinkle with pizza seasoning.

STEP 5
Top with a slice of tomato, followed by the mix of grated cheese and again sprinkle with pizza seasoning.

STEP 6
Bake in the air fryer for 6 minutes until the cheese melts.

STEP 7
Finally, top the mushrooms with pepperoni and cook for another 2 minutes. Remove from the air fryer and enjoy.

BRUSSELS SPROUT AND CHEESE

Cooking Difficulty: 3/10	Cooking Time: 22 minutes	Servings: 2

NUTRITIONAL INFORMATION
Calories: 224, Fat: 18.1g, Protein: 10.1g, Carbs: 4.5g

INGREDIENTS

- ¾ c. brussels sprouts
- 1 tbsp. extra virgin olive oil
- ¼ tsp. salt
- freshly ground black pepper
- ¼ c. grated mozzarella cheese

STEP 1

Cut the Brussels sprouts into halves then place in a bowl.

STEP 2

Drizzle extra virgin olive oil over the Brussels sprouts then sprinkle salt on top. Toss to combine.

STEP 3

Preheat an Air Fryer to 375°F (191°C).

STEP 4

Transfer the seasoned Brussels sprouts to the Air Fryer then cook for 15 minutes.

STEP 5

After 15 minutes, open the Air Fryer and sprinkle grated Mozzarella cheese over the cooked Brussels sprouts.

STEP 6

Cook the Brussels sprouts in the Air Fryer for 5 minutes or until the Mozzarella cheese is melted.

STEP 7

Once it is done, remove from the Air Fryer then transfer to a serving dish. Serve and enjoy.

AVOCADO STICKS

Cooking Difficulty: 2/10	Cooking Time: 10 minutes	Servings: 6

INGREDIENTS

- 2 avocados
- 1 c. coconut flour
- 2 tsps. black pepper
- 3 egg yolks
- 1½ tbsps. water
- ¼ tsp. salt
- 1 c. vegan butter
- 2 tsps. minced garlic
- ¼ c. chopped parsley
- 1 tbsp. lemon juice

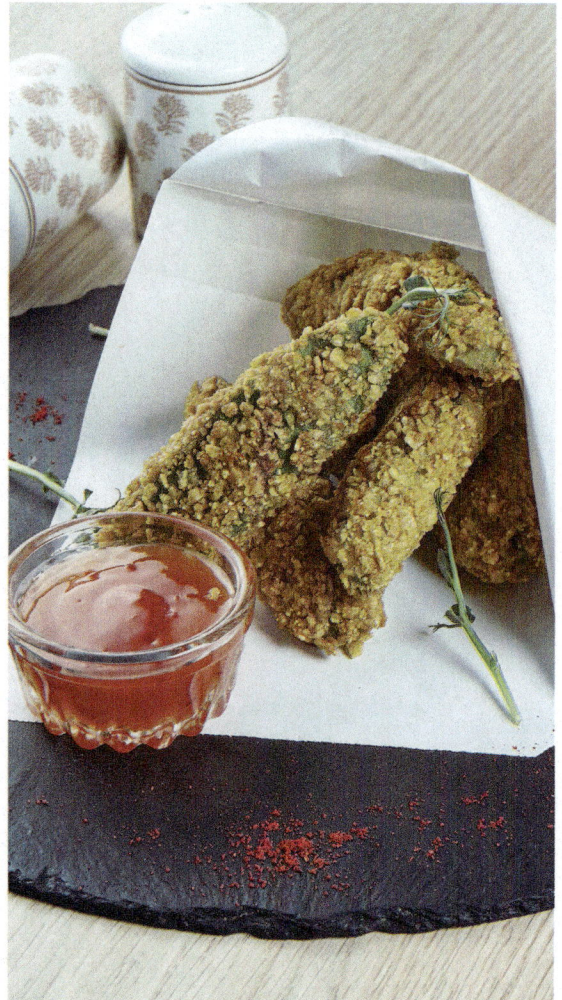

NUTRITIONAL INFORMATION
Calories: 340, Fat: 33.8g, Protein: 4.5g, Carbs: 8.5g

STEP 1

Place butter in a mixing bowl then adds minced garlic, chopped parsley, and lemon juice to the bowl.

STEP 2

Using an electric mixer mix until smooth and fluffy. Transfer the garlic butter to a container with a lid then store in the fridge.

STEP 3

Peel the avocados then cut into wedges. Set aside. Put the egg yolks in a mixing bowl then pour water into it.

STEP 4

Season with salt and black pepper, then stir until incorporated. Take an avocado wedge then roll in the coconut flour.

STEP 5

Dip in the egg mixture then returns back to the coconut flour. Roll until the avocado wedge is completely coated. Repeat with the remaining avocado wedges.

STEP 6

Preheat an Air Fryer to 400°F (204°C). Arrange the coated avocado wedges in the Air Fryer basket then cook for 8 minutes or until golden.

STEP 7

Remove from the Air Fryer then arrange on a serving dish.

STEP 8

Serve with garlic butter then enjoy right away.

FISH & SEAFOOD

for pescetarians

ROASTED GREEN BEANS WITH SHRIMP

Cooking Difficulty: 3/10	Cooking Time: 18 minutes	Servings: 4

NUTRITIONAL INFORMATION
Calories: 300, Fat: 40g, Carbs: 19g, Protein: 72g

INGREDIENTS

green beans:
- 1 lb. green beans, trimmed, cut
- 1½ tbsps. olive oil
- ½ tsp. ground coriander
- ½ tsp. ground cumin
- ½ tsp. salt
- ½ tsp. fresh ground black pepper
- 1/8 tsp. cayenne pepper

shrimp:
- ¾ lb. raw shrimp, peeled
- 1½ tbsps. olive oil
- zest of 1 lemon
- ½ tsp. salt
- ½ tsp. ground black

STEP 1
Preheat the air fryer to 360 °F. Trim your green beans, cut and place in a medium bowl. Add ground coriander, olive oil, ground cumin, salt, and black and cayenne peppers. Toss well to coat.

STEP 2
In a separate bowl, combine the peeled shrimp with olive oil, lemon zest, salt, and freshly ground black pepper.

STEP 3
Coat the air fryer basket with olive oil and spread the beans in it.

STEP 4
Cook for 8 minutes is shaking the basket 1-2 times through the cooking time.

STEP 5
Then top the beans with shelled shrimp and continue cooking for another 10 minutes.

STEP 6
Transfer to a serving dish, drizzle with freshly squeezed lemon juice and serve immediately.

AIR FRIED FISH CAKES

Cooking Difficulty: 3/10	Cooking Time: 9 minutes	Servings: 2

INGREDIENTS

- 2 cod fish filets
- ½ c. flour
- 3 eggs
- 1 tsp. light soy sauce
- 2 cloves garlic
- 3 chopped green onions
- 2 small chilies
- salt and pepper

STEP 1
In a shallow bowl, beat the eggs.

STEP 2
Thinly chop the onions, garlic, and chilies and add to the eggs. Mix well.

STEP 3
Remove the skin of the fish and cut into medium size cubes. Dip your fish cakes in the egg mixture, and then coat them with flour.

STEP 4
Air-fry, the fish pieces at 380 °F for 7 minutes, turning over once through the cooking time.

STEP 5
Serve and enjoy!

NUTRITIONAL INFORMATION
Calories: 369, Fat: 8.1g, Carbs: 27g, Protein: 44.5g

FISH AND LENTIL BURGER PATTIES

![Cooking Difficulty]	Cooking Difficulty: 3/10	![Cooking Time]	Cooking Time: 12 minutes	![Servings]	Servings: 4

NUTRITIONAL INFORMATION
Calories: 276, Fat: 10.1g, Carbs: 23.4g, Protein: 22.7g

INGREDIENTS

- 10 oz. cream dory fillets, steamed and flaked
- 1 c. cooked lentils
- 1 beaten egg
- 1 chopped onion
- 1 red bell pepper, deseeded and chopped
- 1 chopped celery stalk
- 2/3 c. breadcrumbs
- 2 tbsps. chopped cilantro
- 1 tsp. dried thyme
- ½ tsp. garlic powder
- kosher salt
- ground black

STEP 1

In a plate, place cooked dory fillets and use a fork to flake the fish.

STEP 2

In a mixing bowl, mix the flaked dory with the rest of the ingredients. Season with salt and pepper. Mix well.

STEP 3

Scoop about ¼ cup of mixture and form into patties.

STEP 4

Preheat Air Fryer to 390°F.

STEP 5

Place fish 2-3 patties in the Air Fryer cooking basket. Cook until golden brown for approximately 10 minutes. Repeat with remaining patties.

STEP 6

Serve with a fresh salad on the side.

STEP 7

Enjoy!

AIR FRYER CAJUN TUNA STEAKS

Cooking Difficulty: 2/10	Cooking Time: 9 minutes	Servings: 4

INGREDIENTS

- 1 lb. fresh tuna steaks
- 2 tbsps. cajun seasoning

STEP 1
Sprinkle the Cajun seasoning all over the tuna steaks and rub to coat evenly.

STEP 2
Preheat your air fryer to 400 °F.

STEP 3
Arrange the fish pieces in a baking pan, coated with cooking spray and set the timer for 8 minutes.

STEP 4
Flip the fish halfway through the cooking to brown it evenly.

NUTRITIONAL INFORMATION
Calories: 219, Fat: 11g, Carbs: 0g, Protein: 30g

GLAZED SALMON AND VEGETABLE ROAST

Cooking Difficulty: 3/10	Cooking Time: 10 minutes	Servings: 4

NUTRITIONAL INFORMATION
Calories: 290, Fat: 12.4g, Carbs: 16.3g, Protein: 24.2g

INGREDIENTS

- 4 salmon fillets
- 2 diced tomatoes
- 1 red bell pepper, deseeded and chopped
- 1 yellow red bell pepper, deseeded and chopped
- 1 sliced zucchini
- cooking oil spray
- kosher salt
- ground black pepper
  for the marinade:
- ¼ c. mirin
- ¼ c. orange juice
- 2 tbsps. olive oil
- 2 tbsps. soy sauce, low-sodium
- 1 tbsp. lemon juice
- 1 tbsp. honey
- 1 tsp. ground ginger
- 1 tsp. minced garlic

STEP 1

Combine marinade ingredients in a mixing bowl. Mix well. Divide among two shallow bowls.

STEP 2

Add the salmon fillets in one bowl with marinade and the vegetables in another bowl. Toss to coat well. Cover with plastic wrap and let sit in the refrigerator for 30 minutes.

STEP 3

Preheat your Air Fryer to 360°F. Transfer the marinated salmon and place into the Air Fryer cooking basket along with the marinated vegetables. Cook for 8-10 minutes. Serve and enjoy!

AIR FRIED SQUID RINGS

Cooking Difficulty: 2/10	Cooking Time: 10 minutes	Servings: 5

INGREDIENTS

- 1 lb. frozen squid/calamari rings, thawed, washed, and dried
- 1 egg, beaten
- 1 c. all-purpose flour
- 1 tsp. ground coriander seeds
- 1 tsp. cayenne pepper
- ½ tsp. ground black pepper
- ½ tsp. kosher salt
- lemon wedges
- olive oil spray

STEP 1
In a mixing bowl, combine all-purpose flour, paprika, cayenne pepper, salt and ground pepper.

STEP 2
Coat each calamari ring with egg and then flour mixture.

STEP 3
Preheat Air Fryer to 390°F. Place coated calamari rings in the Air Fryer cooking basket. Spray with oil. Cook until browned for about 10 minutes. Cook in batches if needed.

STEP 4
Add lemon wedges for garnish and serve alongside tartar sauce. Enjoy!

NUTRITIONAL INFORMATION
Calories: 238, Fat: 8.9g, Carbs: 22.7g, Protein: 18.4g

AIR FRIED CAJUN SHRIMP

Cooking Difficulty: 2/10	Cooking Time: 7 minutes	Servings: 5

INGREDIENTS

- 1 lb. fresh shrimp
- 2 tbsps. olive oil
- 1 tsp. Spanish paprika
- ½ tsp. garlic powder
- ½ tsp. ground cumin
- ¼ tsp. oregano
- ¼ tsp. thyme
- ¼ tsp. ground black pepper
- ¼ tsp. sea salt

STEP 1
In a bowl, mix all spice ingredients.

STEP 2
Add the shrimps and drizzle with olive oil. Toss to coat well. Cover and place inside the refrigerator to 30 minutes.

STEP 3
Preheat your Air Fryer to 390°F.

STEP 4
Transfer the shrimps into your Air Fryer cooking basket and cook for about 5-7 minutes.

STEP 5
Serve immediately and enjoy!

NUTRITIONAL INFORMATION
Calories: 156, Fat: 7.2 g, Carbs: 3.8 g, Protein: 22.3 g

ROASTED SALMON WITH LEMON AND ROSEMARY

Cooking Difficulty: 2/10	Cooking Time: 10 minutes	Servings: 4

INGREDIENTS

- 4 salmon steak
- 1 tbsps. olive oil
- 2 tbsps. lemon juice
- 1 tsp. garlic, minced
- 2 tbsps. freshly chopped rosemary
- himalayan salt
- freshly ground black pepper

STEP 1

In a dish mix garlic, olive oil, rosemary, and lemon juice; add the salmon steaks and rub with a mixture. Cover and let it sit inside the refrigerator for 30 minutes.

STEP 2

Preheat your Air Fryer to 390°F.

STEP 3

Place the marinated salmon steaks in cooking basket and cook for about 8-10 minutes.

STEP 4

Transfer into a serving dish. Garnish with fresh rosemary leaves. Serve and enjoy!

NUTRITIONAL INFORMATION

Calories: 209, Fat: 12.1 g, Carbs: 2.3 g, Protein: 22.4 g

DESSERTS & SNACKS

BREADED JALAPENO POPPERS

Cooking Difficulty: 2/10	Cooking Time: 10 minutes	Servings: 8

INGREDIENTS

- 16 pcs. medium sized jalapenos
- olive oil spray

for the breading:

- 1 c. all-purpose flour
- 2 beaten whole eggs
- 1 c. breadcrumbs
- ½ tsp. kosher salt
- ¼ tsp. ground black pepper

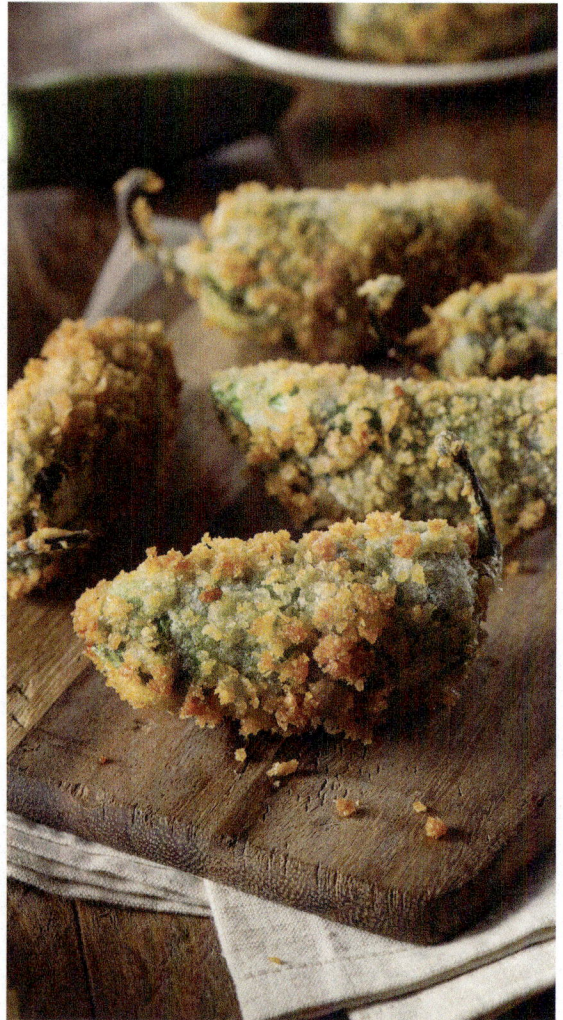

NUTRITIONAL INFORMATION
Calories: 164, Fat: 6.6g, Carbs: 23.2g, Protein: 5.1g

STEP 1

Wash the jalapenos under running water. Dry them with paper towels.

STEP 2

In a mixing bowl, place flour then season with salt and pepper.

STEP 3

Place beaten eggs and breadcrumbs in separate bowls.

STEP 4

Coat the jalapenos in seasoned flour, and then beaten eggs, and lastly in breadcrumbs.

STEP 5

Preheat your Air Fryer to 390°F.

STEP 6

Arrange breaded jalapenos in the cooking basket such that it is not too overcrowded. Spray with oil.

STEP 7

Cook for 7-10 minutes or until breadcrumbs turns golden brown.

STEP 8

Serve hot with your favorite dipping sauce and enjoy!

APPLE CINNAMON CRUMBLE WITH ALMOND

🧑‍🍳 Cooking Difficulty: 4/10	⏰ Cooking Time: 40 minutes	🍽 Servings: 6

NUTRITIONAL INFORMATION
Calories: 334, Fat: 14g, Carbs: 51g, Protein: 5g

INGREDIENTS

for the stewed apples:
- 1½ lbs. apples, peeled, halved and cored
- 1 c. water
- 1/3 c. brown sugar
- 1 tsp. ground cinnamon

for the crumble:
- 4 oz. vegan butter
- 4 oz. flour
- 3 oz. ground almonds
- 3 oz. oats
- 1 tsp. cinnamon powder

STEP 1
Preheat your Air Fryer to 360°F.

STEP 2
Cut the apples into small pieces.

STEP 3
In a large saucepan, heat ¾ cup of water and bring to a simmer. Add the apple chunks, brown sugar, and cinnamon. Cook, stirring for about 10 minutes or until apples are softened and a sauce has become thick. Set aside.

STEP 4
In a food processor, process all ingredients for the crumble until combined well, and the texture turns crumbly.

STEP 5
Place the stewed apples into a baking dish that can fit into the Air Fryer cooking basket. Then, top apples with crumble mixture. Cook for 25-30 minutes, or until golden brown. Let cool.

STEP 6
Divide among 6 serving bowls. Serve and enjoy!

SWEET POTATO FRIES WITH BASIL

Cooking Difficulty: 2/10	Cooking Time: 25 minutes	Servings: 6

INGREDIENTS

- 6 sweet potatoes, sliced
- ¼ c. olive oil
- 2 tbsps. chopped basil leaves, fresh
- 5g sweet paprika
- ½ tsp. sea salt
- ½ tsp. black pepper

STEP 1
Soak the sweet potatoes in water for at least 30 minutes. Drain thoroughly and pat dry with paper towel.

STEP 2
Preheat your Air Fryer to 360°F. Combine the olive oil, basil, paprika, salt, and pepper in a large bowl. Add the sliced sweet potatoes. Toss to coat well.

STEP 3
Transfer the sweet potatoes into the cooking basket and cook until browned for about 25 minutes. Garnish with basil leaves. Serve and enjoy!

NUTRITIONAL INFORMATION
Calories: 221, Fat: 9.2g, Carbs: 35g, Protein: 2.1g

ZUCCHINI WEDGES WITH MARINARA SAUCE

 Cooking Difficulty: 3/10

 Cooking Time: 45 minutes

 Servings: 8

INGREDIENTS

- 4 sized zucchini, sliced
  for the breading:
- 1 c. all-purpose flour
- 2 whole eggs, beaten
- ½ tsp. kosher salt
- ¼ tsp. ground black pepper
  for the marinara sauce:
- 2 tbsps. olive oil
- 1 tbsp. (10 g) garlic, minced
- ½ c. chopped onion
- 28 oz. canned crushed tomatoes
- ½ tsp. dried oregano leaves
- ½ tsp. dried parsley
- ½ tsp. sweet paprika

NUTRITIONAL INFORMATION

Calories: 365, Fat: 34.6g, Protein: 10.4g, Carbs: 4.4g

STEP 1

Make the marinara sauce by heating olive oil a small sauce pan.

STEP 2

Sauté onions and garlic until fragrant.

STEP 3

Mix in crushed tomatoes, oregano leaves, parsley, and cayenne pepper. Stir together. Add in parmesan cheese. Turn the heat to low and simmer the sauce for about 30 minutes.

STEP 4

As the marinara sauce is being cooked. Prepare the zucchini wedges. In a mixing bowl, place all-purpose flour and season with salt and pepper.

STEP 5

Place beaten eggs in a separate bowl. Coat zucchini wedges first in seasoned flour and then beaten eggs.

STEP 6

Preheat your Air Fryer to 390°F. Arrange coated zucchini wedges in a cooking basket without them being too crowded. Spray lightly with oil.

STEP 7

Cook until golden brown for approximately 10 minutes.

STEP 8

Turn off the burner and transfer marinara sauce into a serving bowl.

STEP 9

Serve with zucchini wedges. Enjoy!

AIR FRIED PUMPKIN CHIPS

Cooking Difficulty: 2/10	Cooking Time: 20 minutes	Servings: 6

NUTRITIONAL INFORMATION
Calories: 195, Fat: 9.4g, Carbs: 19.3g, Protein: 9.5g

INGREDIENTS

- 1½ lbs. pumpkin, peeled
- 3 tbsps. olive oil
- ½ tsp. ground coriander seeds
- ½ tsp. paprika
- ¼ tsp. sea salt
- ¼ tsp. black pepper

STEP 1
Preheat your Hot Air Fryer to 360°F.

STEP 2
Slice pumpkin into ¼-inch thick cuts and use round 2-inch diameter cookie-cutter to produce round pumpkin chips.

STEP 3
In a bowl, mix ground coriander, sea salt, olive oil, and pepper. Mix well.

STEP 4
Add the sliced pumpkin into the mixture and toss, making sure every chip is coated well.

STEP 5
Place the coated pumpkin slices in the Air Fryer cooking basket. Cook until browned and crisp in batches if needed for about 20 minutes.

STEP 6
Serve with your favorite dipping sauce.

STEP 7
Enjoy!

BRUSCHETTA WITH PESTO CHEESE AND TOMATO

	Cooking Difficulty: 2/10		Cooking Time: 6 minutes		Servings: 6

INGREDIENTS

- 1 loaf baguette, sliced crosswise into 12 slices
- 1 c. sliced cherry tomatoes
- 4 oz. mozzarella cheese, shredded
- ¾ c. prepared pesto
- ¼ c. basil leaves, coarsely chopped

STEP 1
Preheat Air Fryer to 390°F.

STEP 2
To one side of baguette, spread pesto sauce and top with mozzarella and then with sliced cherry tomatoes.

STEP 3
Place bruschetta in the Air Fryer cooking basket and cook for 3-5 minutes. Sprinkle with fresh basil.

STEP 4
Transfer bruschetta into a serving dish.

STEP 5
Serve and enjoy!

NUTRITIONAL INFORMATION
Calories: 216, Fat: 8.2g, Carbs: 27g, Protein: 9g

AIR-FRIED MOZZARELLA STICKS WITH SESAME SEEDS

Cooking Difficulty: 2/10	Cooking Time: 10 minutes	Servings: 8

NUTRITIONAL INFORMATION
Calories: 195, Fat: 9.4g, Carbs: 19.3g, Protein: 9.5g

INGREDIENTS

- 16 oz. mozzarella cheese, sliced
- 2 beaten whole eggs
- 165g Japanese breadcrumbs
- 2/3 c. all-purpose flour
- ½ tsp. ground coriander seed
- ½ tsp. kosher salt
- ¼ tsp. ground black pepper
- 2 tbsps. sesame seeds
- cooking oil spray

STEP 1
In a bowl, combine pepper, coriander, all-purpose flour, and salt.

STEP 2
Prepare ingredients by placing beaten eggs, all-purpose flour mixture, breadcrumbs and sesame seeds in separate bowls.

STEP 3
Coat mozzarella sticks first in all-purpose flour mixture, then beaten eggs, breadcrumbs, and sesame seeds.

STEP 4
Preheat your Air Fryer to 390°F.

STEP 5
Arrange the coated mozzarella sticks in the Air Fryer cooking basket, be careful not to overcrowd.

STEP 6
Cook mozzarella sticks until browned for 10 minutes.

STEP 7
Serve with your choice of dipping sauce and enjoy!

SPICED POTATO CHIP WITH GARLIC YOGURT DIP

STEP 1
Preheat your Hot Air Fryer to 390°F.

STEP 2
In a mixing bowl, combine the olive oil, salt, pepper, and nutmeg. Mix well.

STEP 3
Add the sliced potatoes to mixture and toss, making sure every potato slice is coated well.

STEP 4
Arrange coated potato slices in the Air Fryer basket and cook in batches to avoid overcrowding.

STEP 5
Cook each batch for about 15 minutes or until crisp and golden brown.

STEP 6
As the potato chips are being cooked, prepare the garlic yogurt dip.

STEP 7
In a mortar and pestle, combine garlic, and salt then crushes together. Transfer this mixture into a small bowl. Add yogurt and lemon juice. Season with pepper. Refrigerate until ready to serve.

STEP 8
Once all the potato chips have been cooked, serve with garlic yogurt dip. Enjoy!

 Cooking Difficulty: 3/10	 Cooking Time: 17 minutes	 Servings: 4

INGREDIENTS

- 4 potatoes, cleaned and sliced
- 2 tbsps. olive oil
- ½ tsp. sea salt
- ½ tsp. black pepper
- ½ tsp. nutmeg, grated

for the garlic yogurt dip:
- 1 tsp. crushed garlic
- ¼ tsp. sea salt
- ¼ tsp. ground black pepper
- 6 oz. plain greek yogurt
- 1 tbsp. fresh lemon juice

NUTRITIONAL INFORMATION
Calories: 174, Fat: 8g, Carbs: 20.2g, Protein: 6.3g

MINTY PUMPKIN BOMBS

Cooking Difficulty: 3/10	Cooking Time: 15 minutes	Servings: 4

INGREDIENTS

- ¾ lb. pumpkin
- ¼ c. chopped onion
- ¼ c. chopped parsley, dill
- 1 c. roasted pecans
- 2 tsps. chopped mint leaves
- ¼ c. almond flour
- 1 tsp. thyme
- 1½ tbsp. mustard
- ½ tsp. salt
- ½ tsp. pepper
- ¼ lb. mozzarella cheese
- 2 egg

NUTRITIONAL INFORMATION
Calories: 438, Fat: 41.3g, Protein: 12g, Carbs: 9.9g

STEP 1

Peel the pumpkin then cut into cubes.

STEP 2

Place the cubed pumpkin in a food processor then process until smooth.

STEP 3

Transfer the smooth pumpkin to a bowl then add chopped onion, parsley, dill, mint leaves, and flour. Season with thyme, mustard, salt, and pepper. Mix until combined.

STEP 4

Shape the pumpkin mixture into small balls the fill each ball with Mozzarella cheese. Arrange the pumpkin balls on a tray then refrigerate for 15 minutes.

STEP 5

Meanwhile, place the roasted pecans in a food processor then process until smooth and becoming crumbles. Set aside. In a separate bowl, crack the egg then using a fork stir until incorporated.

STEP 6

Preheat an Air Fryer to 400°F (204°C). Take the pumpkin bowl out of the refrigerator then dip in the egg.

STEP 7

Roll the pumpkin balls in the pecan crumbles then arrange on the Air Fryer's rack.

STEP 8

Cook the pumpkin balls for 12 minutes then remove from heat. Serve and enjoy warm.

PEACH WITH CINNAMON DESSERT

Cooking Difficulty: 2/10	Cooking Time: 7 minutes	Servings: 4

INGREDIENTS

- 4 ripe peaches, stoned and quartered
- 1 tbsp. lemon juice
- 1 tsp. cinnamon powder

STEP 1
Preheat Air Fryer to 360°F.

STEP 2
Coat all peaches with cinnamon powder.

STEP 3
Place the peaches in the Air Fryer cooking basket and cook for 5-7 minutes.

STEP 4
Transfer into a serving dish. Drizzle with lemon juice.

STEP 5
Serve and enjoy!

NUTRITIONAL INFORMATION
Calories: 216, Fat: 8.2g, Carbs: 27g, Protein: 9g

COCONUT CHEESECAKE

	Cooking Difficulty: 4/10		Cooking Time: 20 minutes		Servings: 8

INGREDIENTS

- ¾ c. almond flour
- ¾ c. coconut flour
- ½ c. grated coconut
- ¾ c. vegan butter
- 3 c. cream cheese
- 1 c. sour cream
- 5 tbsps. Stevia
- 4 eggs
- 1 tsp. lemon zest
- ½ tsp. vanillin

NUTRITIONAL INFORMATION

Calories: 365, Fat: 34.6g, Protein: 10.4g, Carbs: 4.4g

STEP 1

Prepare a spring-form pan that fits the Air Fryer.

STEP 2

Allow butter to melt in the microwave then combine with almond flour, coconut flour, vanillin and grated coconut. Mix until becoming dough. Place the dough in the prepared spring-form pan then spread evenly.

STEP 3

Press to the bottom of the spring-form pan then store in the fridge. Meanwhile, place cream cheese in a mixing bowl then using an electric mixer beat the cream cheese until soft and fluffy.

STEP 4

Add sour cream, stevia, eggs, and lemon zest to the bowl then beat again until incorporated and fluffy.

STEP 5

Remove the spring-form pan from the fridge then pour the filling over the base. Spread evenly.

STEP 6

Preheat an Air Fryer to 180°F (82°C). Place the spring-form pan in the Air Fryer then cook for 15 minutes.

STEP 7

Remove the cheesecake from the Air Fryer then let it cool. Once the cheesecake is cool, store in the fridge for at least 6 hours. Serve and enjoy cold.

CONCLUSION

Trying to lose weight will always look like a test because it is a change that does not come fast. People are ready to try out any type of diet that promises them miraculous slimming within a week or so without thinking that losing weight should be a healthy and steady process.

The vegetarian diet is followed by millions of people around the world. It is not a new thing; it exists for as long there is human life on this planet. Some people switch to plant-based meals because they are empathetic and do not want to pay for the murder of an innocent animal and eat their dead body. Others become vegetarians because they want to eat healthily (meat is known to contain additives and hormones). Among the many reasons, there is the price of the meat (it can be quite expensive for some people), health issues, or simply because some people want to purify their bodies.

If you want to switch the vegetarianism for whatever reason, and you wonder if you could lose weight with this diet, the answer is affirmative.

Vegetarianism offers you a plethora of healthy foods that are rich in vitamins, minerals, fiber, proteins, carbs, and healthy fats.

The key to losing weight while following this diet is to create the 40-30-30 ratio in your plate; have 40 percent of carbs and 30 percent for proteins and fats.

Instead of indulging in unhealthy vegetarian options that are packed with saturated fats, sodium, and sugar, always go for the options that contain fresh ingredients such as vegetables, fruits, nuts, healthy oils (olive oil).

There are several types of the vegetarian diet, and you can pick the one that works best for you. It is up to you to pick a type of this diet, combine it with fish, eggs, and dairy products, or become a vegan.

The key to slim while following the vegetarian diet is to control your calorie intake and be mindful of the food you eat.

Start reading the labels on your food. Create a weekly menu and prepare your meals in advance. This way, you will always know what you eat and how many calories you consumed.

And of course, any diet combined with physical activities will show great results. Do not forget to exercise while cutting down your calories.

The workout type can vary from swimming, cycling, hiking, working out at the gym, or simply walking to school or work every day.

And finally, if you want to try another challenge while following this diet, you can combine it with intermittent fasting.

Once you adapt to the scheduled eating (pick the method that works best for you), you will see that intermittent fasting is an excellent diet plan that works like a charm with any diet.

I hope that this book helped you learn something more about the vegetarian diet (especially for the foods that are rich in iron, proteins, healthy fats, and fiber, as well as the foods that are suppressing your cravings).

Switching to any diet can be a challenge, but at the end of the day, we should win the "battle" against our own minds, rather than believe that we are not disciplined or dedicated enough to lose several kilograms.

If you are about to give the vegetarian diet a try, I wish you a happy start.

Thank you for spending your time to read this book.

Garry Goodman

Printed in Great Britain
by Amazon